Selections from Aunt Sammy's Radio Recipes and USDA Favorites

Aunt Sammy came to life with the first radio broadcast of "Housekeeper's Chat" on October 4, 1926. The character of Aunt Sammy—wife of Uncle Sam—was created by the USDA Bureau of Home Economics and the Radio Service. Many women across the country played the part as they spoke into the microphones of local radio stations.

The highlights of Aunt Sammy's show were the menus and recipes, but Aunt Sammy also talked about clothing, furniture, appliances, and other family and household matters. Aunt Sammy wasn't just a homebody, however. She commented on world affairs, reported the latest fads, and told jokes. The talk moved easily from one subject to another, always natural and entertaining as well as informative.

Aunt Sammy soon became popular. By the end of the first year her program was carried by 43 radio stations. By 1932, 194 stations were broadcasting Aunt Sammy's show. A number of the stations were broadcasting the show five times a week.

Many listeners wrote for copies of the recipes, and the Bureau of Home Economics answered these requests with weekly mimeographed sheets. In 1927 the most popular recipes were assembled into a pamphlet. The demand was so great that it had to be reprinted after only a month. "Aunt

Sammy's Radio Recipes" was revised and enlarged three times between 1927 and 1931. In 1932 it became the first cookbook published in braille.

Aunt Sammy faded out during the Great Depression. After 1934 the name Aunt Sammy was no longer used. The radio show became drier and more factual and was renamed "Homemaker Chats." In 1946 it was discontinued.

Today, consumers are still looking to USDA for information on how to make the best use of the food available to them. A research program in the Consumer and Food Economics Institute of the Science and Education Administration provides the basis for numerous laboratory-tested recipes.

Current recipes emphasize time-saving techniques, moneysaving ingredients, and good nutrition. Taste panels are used to evaluate new recipes.

Research has provided a group of publications for the consumer on specific foods such as fruits, vegetables, eggs, beef, poultry, cheese, milk, and soybeans. The series is designed to give information about buying, storing, and using specific commodities. These and other publications help consumers use a wide variety of foods to obtain nutritious, appetizing, and economical meals.

Providing directions for home canning and freezing is another service of the Consumer and Food Economics Institute. Publications give safe procedures for preserving fruits, vegetables, meats, and poultry. Many thousands of these publications have been distributed to consumers, and the procedures have been widely used by others who make recommendations to the public about food preservation. Still other publications tell how to store food properly for maximum quality and safety.

This 50th anniversary recipe collection includes recipes from current publications and a selection of recipes from the first edition of "Aunt Sammy's Radio Recipes." All of these recipes have been retested in the laboratory and found acceptable by taste panels.

Soups

Onion Soup Au Gratin

3 cups meat broth.
6 medium-sized onions, chopped.
½ teaspoon salt.
4 tablespoons flour.
2 tablespoons cold water.
Pepper.
Toast.
Parmesan cheese.

Cook the chopped onions in a small amount of water until tender. Add 2 tablespoons of fat from the meat broth or the same quantity of butter and let the onions cook down in this until they are yellow. Mix them with the meat broth and salt and thicken with the flour and cold water which have been blended. Cook for a few minutes. Season with pepper as desired. Pour the soup into bowls or soup plates, place on top a round or slice of toasted bread, and sprinkle grated cheese over the bread and soup. Serve at once.

Milk-Vegetable Soups

Milk-vegetable soups are made from cooked vegetables (chopped or sliced) and milk slightly thickened. The vegetables may be asparagus, peas, beans of various kinds, celery, potatoes, turnips, carrots, spinach, onions, corn, cabbage, or almost any other vegetable. Some of these are good in combination, such as potatoes and onions, potatoes and turnips, turnips and carrots.

2 cups milk.
1 tablespoon flour or less.
1 tablespoon butter.
Salt.

⅔ cup cooked vegetables, finely chopped, mashed or strained.

Thicken the milk with the flour as for white sauce. Add the other ingredients. If the vegetable is starchy, use less flour or thin the soup with milk. The vegetables should be finely chopped, mashed, or strained, so that they will blend well with the thickened milk.

Main Dishes

Shepherd's Pie

Grease a 2-quart baking dish and cover the sides with a thin layer of seasoned mashed potato. Use about 2½ cups potato. Fill the center with about 4½ cups well-seasoned, slightly thickened stew, creamed chicken, or creamed fish. There should be no potatoes in the stew. Cover the top with 1 cup mashed potato and bake in a hot oven (400°F.) until the pie is hot through and slightly browned on top.

NOTE: The recipe for Beef Stew on page 13 may be used.

Fricasseed Chicken with Dumplings

Cut chicken into pieces for serving. Roll each piece in flour and brown in hot fat. Browning the chicken before cooking it helps retain and develop the flavor. After the pieces are browned, simmer until tender in enough water to cover. When it is done, take the chicken out and cook dumplings in the gravy. Serve the chicken in the center of a platter with the dumplings around the edge. Pour the gravy over the chicken.

Dumplings

1 cup flour.
2½ teaspoons baking powder.
½ teaspoon salt.
1 egg.
⅓ cup milk.

Sift the flour, baking powder and salt together. Beat the egg well, add the milk, and mix with the dry ingredients. Drop by small spoonfuls into the chicken gravy. Cover tightly and cook for 15 minutes. The top must not be removed while the dumplings are cooking. If the steam escapes, the dumplings will not be light.

Baked Cheese and Macaroni

2 cups macaroni or spaghetti, broken in small pieces.
4 tablespoons flour.
4 tablespoons butter.
2 cups milk.
¾ pound American cheese.
1 teaspoon salt.
Butter.
Soft bread crumbs.

Cook the macaroni or spaghetti in 2 quarts of boiling salted water until tender. Drain. Make a sauce with the flour, butter, milk, and salt. Grate or cut the cheese into the sauce, reserving a little to grate over the top of the dish.

Place the macaroni in a buttered baking dish, in alternate layers with the cheese sauce. Scatter the extra grated cheese over the top with buttered bread crumbs. Bake in a moderate oven (350°F.) until the sauce and macaroni are hot through and the crumbs are brown.

Smothered Ham with Sweetpotatoes

1 slice of smoked ham, cut into sizes for serving.
3 cups raw, sliced sweetpotatoes.
1 tablespoon butter or ham drippings.
2 tablespoons sugar.
1 cup hot water.

Brown the ham lightly on both sides and arrange it to cover the bottom of a baking dish. Spread the sliced sweetpotatoes over the ham. Sprinkle with sugar. Add the hot water and fat. Cover the dish and bake slowly at 350°F. (moderate oven) until the ham is tender. Baste the potatoes occasionally with the liquid. Brown the top well.

Creamed Oysters

1 quart oysters.
2½ cups milk and oyster liquor.
½ cup butter.
½ cup flour.
1 teaspoon salt.
⅛ teaspoon pepper.
¼ teaspoon onion juice, if desired.

Cook the oysters in their liquor until the edges begin to curl. Do not let them cook too long or they will be tough. Strain off the liquor. To about 1 cup of this liquor, add enough milk to make 2½ cups. Melt the butter and add the flour, stirring until blended. Add the liquid. Cook for 5 or 10 minutes to do away with the starchy flavor of the flour. Add the oysters and seasoning and serve at once in patty shells or on toast. If creamed oysters stand, the sauce becomes thin.

Vegetables

Harvard Beets

6 medium-sized beets.
½ cup sugar.
½ tablespoon cornstarch.
½ cup vinegar.
2 tablespoons butter.

Wash beets, cook in boiling water until tender, remove the skins, and cut the beets into thin slices or cubes. Mix the sugar and cornstarch. Add the vinegar, and let the sauce boil for 5 minutes, stirring constantly. Just as the sauce is taken from the fire add the butter. Pour sauce over beets. Let them stand on the back of the stove for a few minutes so that the beets may absorb the sweet-sour flavor of the sauce.

Baked Cucumbers

3 good-sized cucumbers.
¾ cup fine dry breadcrumbs.
3 tablespoons butter.
½ teaspoon salt.
1½ tablespoons chopped onion.
1½ teaspoons finely chopped parsley.
1 tablespoon chopped celery.
1 cup tomatoes cut in pieces.

Wash cucumbers and cut in half lengthwise. Scoop out as much as possible of the pulp without breaking the skin. Brown the onion in the fat, add other ingredients mixed with the cucumber pulp. Stir constantly, and cook five minutes, or until dry. Place the filling in the cucumber shells and bake until the shells are soft and the mixture is brown on top.

Browned Parsnips

Scrub parsnips clean, drop into boiling, lightly salted water, and cook for 15 to 30 minutes or until tender. Drain, scrape off the skin, split lengthwise, and pull out the stringy cores. Dip the pieces in flour and fry in fat until golden brown.

Corn Fritters

1 cup liquid, either juice from canned corn or milk, or the two mixed.
1 cup drained canned corn.
1¾ cups sifted cake flour
1 tablespoon melted fat.
1 egg.
2 teaspoons baking powder.
¾ teaspoon salt.

Mix the flour, baking powder, and salt. Mix the juice from the canned corn or milk, or whatever liquid is used, the egg after it has been beaten slightly, and the canned corn. Stir this liquid mixture gradually into the dry ingredients. Add the melted fat. If the corn is very moist, even after the liquid has been drained from it, more flour may be needed.

Fry the corn fritters in deep fat, or if preferred, in a skillet in shallow fat. In either case, drop the mixture by spoonfuls into the fat and fry rather slowly. The fritters need time to cook through to the center before the outside becomes too brown. Drain the fritters on absorbent paper and serve hot.

Scalloped Onions and Peanuts

6 medium-sized onions.
½ cup peanuts, ground.
1 cup thin white sauce, made with 1 tablespoon flour, 1 tablespoon butter, and 1 cup milk.

Cook the skinned onions in boiling water until tender. Drain and slice with a sharp knife. Place the onions in layers in a greased baking dish, cover each layer with the cream sauce and the peanuts, and continue until all ingredients are used. Cover the top with buttered crumbs and bake in a moderate oven (350°F.) until golden brown. Serve from the baking dish.

Fruits

Fried Apples and Bacon

Select about six good tart apples. Peel them. Cut them in 1-inch cubes. Fry the bacon in a heavy skillet. As soon as the slices of bacon are crisp, remove and drain them on clean brown paper and keep in a warm place. Leave about one-fourth cup bacon fat in the skillet and fill it with apples. Sprinkle on 3 tablespoons of sugar. Apples fried this way require a little more sugar than ordinary fried apples. Cover the apples. Cook slowly until tender. Then remove the cover and turn apples gently, so the pieces will keep their shape. Let them brown lightly. They are then almost transparent. Place them on a hot platter, and surround them with the crisp bacon.

Scalloped Apples

Pare, core, and slice tart apples, preferably those of a kind that will hold their shape when cooked. Place a layer of the sliced apples in a baking dish, sprinkle with sugar, dot with butter, or pour on a little melted butter. Put in another layer of apples and keep on until the dish is heaping full. Press the apples down and put in as many as possible. Cover the dish and cook the apples slowly for 1 to 1½ hours in a 300°F. (slow) oven. Fifteen minutes before the apples are to be served, remove the cover and spread buttered bread crumbs over the top. Return to the oven and let the crumbs become golden brown and crisp. The apples themselves will be in whole pieces and almost transparent. Some kinds will be pink in color. Scalloped apples are good served hot with main course of dinner or supper.

Salads

Cabbage and Carrot Salad

Use equal parts of grated carrots and finely shredded cabbage. Mix the carrots and cabbage together with salad dressing until well blended. Serve on crisp lettuce.

Stuffed Celery

Cut the celery into pieces convenient for handling. Fill the hollow of the celery stalks with cream cheese mixed with chopped pimiento, green pepper, and chopped nuts. Serve on the plate with another salad or as a relish.

Potato Salad

4 medium-sized potatoes.
1 cup finely cut celery.
1½ teaspoons salt.
1 teaspoon grated onion or more.
¼ cup chopped pickle.
1 cup salad dressing.

Cook the potatoes in their jackets in boiling salted water. As soon as the potatoes are tender, but not soft, drain them and remove the skins. When they are cold, cut the potatoes in small uniform cubes. Add the celery, onion, pickle, salt, and salad dressing. Mix together lightly to avoid breaking the potatoes and making them mushy. Chill thoroughly and serve on crisp lettuce leaves.

Tomato Aspic Salad

2 envelopes gelatin.
1 quart canned tomatoes.
1 tablespoon finely chopped green pepper.
2 tablespoons finely chopped celery.
1 tablespoon finely chopped parsley.
1 cup very finely shredded cabbage.
1½ teaspoons salt.
½ teaspoon onion juice.
½ teaspoon sugar.

Soak the gelatin in a small quantity of water. Boil the tomatoes for 5 minutes and strain through a fine sieve to remove the seeds. Pour the hot tomato juice over the gelatin and stir until it is dissolved. Add the salt, onion juice, and the sugar and chill. When the gelatin mixture is partly set, add the finely shredded vegetables and mix well. Add more salt if needed. Pour into wet custard cups and place in the cold until set. Turn these molds out on crisp lettuce leaves and serve with mayonnaise.

Breads

Boston Brown Bread

1 cup corn meal.
1 cup rye meal.
1 cup whole wheat flour.
1 teaspoon salt.
¾ cup molasses.
2 cups sour milk and 1½ teaspoons soda, or 1¾ cups sweet milk and 4 teaspoons baking powder.

Mix and sift the dry ingredients; add the molasses and the milk. Beat the mixture thoroughly. Pour the batter into a greased tin can or mold until it is about three-fourths full. Cover, and steam for 3½ hours. Remove the cover, and bake the bread in a moderate oven for ½ hour to dry it off. If the bread seems likely to crumble, loop a clean string around the loaf and cut slices by pulling the ends of the string.

Cheese Straws

1 cup flour.
½ teaspoon salt.
¼ cup fat.
1 cup grated cheese.
$1/16$ teaspoon cayenne.
3 tablespoons water.

Cut the flour, salt, cayenne, fat, and one-half of the cheese together with a biscuit cutter until the mass is well blended. Add the water and mix well. Toss on a slightly floured board and roll 2 or 3 times until the dough is smooth. Sprinkle on one half of the remainder of the cheese and roll again. Repeat this until all the cheese is used. Roll the mass out until about ¼ inch thick. Cut in strips ½ inch wide and 6 inches long. Place the strips on a baking sheet and bake until a delicate brown, in a hot oven, about 400°F.

Waffles

1½ cups milk.
2 cups sifted cake flour.
3 tablespoons fat.
2 eggs.
3 teaspoons baking powder.
1½ tablespoons sugar.
¾ teaspoon salt.

Mix the dry ingredients, add the milk and egg yolks, then the melted fat, and lastly fold in the beaten whites of eggs. Have the waffle iron hot enough to brown the waffle quickly and well greased unless it is the electrically heated aluminum kind. In that case, add an extra tablespoon of melted shortening to the batter.

Desserts

Chocolate Souffle

½ cup sugar.
½ cup fine dry bread crumbs.
1 tablespoon flour.
1 tablespoon butter.
1½ squares unsweetened chocolate.
½ teaspoon salt.
¾ cup milk.
4 eggs.
½ teaspoon vanilla.

Mix the flour and butter, add the milk, and stir over heat until thickened. Melt the chocolate over steam, and add to the cream sauce, with the salt, bread crumbs, sugar, vanilla, and well beaten egg yolks. Beat well. Fold in the well beaten whites of the eggs. Pour into a greased 1½ quart pudding dish and bake in a slow oven (325°F.) for 1 hour, or until well set in the middle. Serve hot with the hard sauce (page 9).

Hard Sauce

¼ cup butter.
¾ cup powdered sugar.
½ teaspoon vanilla.
⅛ teaspoon grated nutmeg.

Cream together the butter and sugar, add the vanilla and nutmeg. The secret of creamy hard sauce lies in long beating. Chill before serving.

Rocks

1½ cups light brown sugar.
1 cup butter.
3 eggs, well beaten.

½ teaspoon soda in a little hot water.
1 teaspoon cinnamon.
3 cups raisins, chopped.
1 cup English walnut meats, chopped.
2¾ cups flour.
½ teaspoon salt.

Cream the butter and sugar and add the eggs. Sift the dry ingredients, reserving some flour to roll the raisins and nuts. Mix all together. Place by teaspoonfuls on a greased pan and bake in a hot oven (375°F.).

Baked Caramel Custard

1 quart milk.
5 eggs.
½ cup sugar.
½ teaspoon vanilla.
¼ cup caramel sirup.
¼ teaspoon salt.
Butter.

Heat the milk slightly with the sugar, salt, and caramel sirup. Be sure the caramel sirup is entirely dissolved before this mixture is poured into the lightly beaten eggs. Add the vanilla. Pour the mixture into custard cups, and add a small piece of butter to each. Bake in a pan surrounded by water in a slow oven (325°F.). Test by placing the point of a knife in the center of the custard and if it comes out clean remove the cups of custard at once from the hot water. The custards may be served either hot or cold with caramel sirup if more caramel flavor is desired.

Sugar can be caramelized easily by placing it in a heavy skillet over slow even heat, and stirring it constantly until it melts and becomes a heavy brown sirup. As soon as it reaches this stage take it from the fire at once, and use it for flavoring and sweetening the custard.

Apple Dumplings

Roll the pastry in a thin sheet and cut it in rounds. Place a whole, cored apple in center of each round of pastry.

Sprinkle sugar over the apple, dot with butter, and bring the edges of the pastry together over the apple. Bake in muffin pans, in a moderate oven (350°F.) until apple is tender, about 1 hour. Serve hot with hard sauce (page 9).

Sour Cream Pie

1 cup sour cream.
1 cup sugar.
1 cup seeded raisins, cut fine.
2 eggs.
½ teaspoon powdered cinnamon.
½ teaspoon powdered cloves.
⅛ teaspoon salt.
2 tablespoons vinegar.

Beat the eggs. Mix the spices with the sugar, and add to the eggs with the raisins, cream, salt, and vinegar. Beat well. Pour the mixture into a deep, pastry-lined pie pan. Moisten the outer rim of the pastry, and press the top crust over the lower one to hold in the custard. Bake in a moderate oven (350°F.) until golden brown.

Date Pudding

1½ cups pitted dates.
½ cup milk.
1 cup chopped nuts.
1 cup sugar.
3 eggs.
1 cup flour.
2 tablespoons butter.
1 teaspoon vanilla.
1 teaspoon baking powder.
¼ teaspoon salt.

Mix the butter and sugar and add the beaten eggs and milk. Sift the dry ingredients and add them to the liquid mixture, reserving enough flour to coat the dates and nuts. Add them and the vanilla. Bake in a shallow greased pan in a very slow oven (250°F.) for 1 hour 45 minutes, until set in the center. Cut in squares and serve with whipped cream.

Pumpkin Pie

1½ cups cooked pumpkin.
1 cup milk.
½ cup sugar.
1 teaspoon cinnamon.
½ teaspoon salt.
½ teaspoon allspice.
¼ teaspoon mace.
2 eggs.
1 tablespoon butter.

Put all the ingredients, except the eggs and the butter, in the double boiler. Bring to the scalding point. Beat eggs well; stir a small amount of hot mixture into the eggs; stir egg mixture into the remaining hot mixture. Stir until it starts to thicken. Add the butter. Line a pie pan with pastry and bake until light brown. Pour the hot filling into a baked crust. Bake the pie in a moderately hot oven (400°F.) until the filling sets.

Applesauce Cake

1 cup sugar.
½ cup fat.
1 cup applesauce, unsweetened.
1 cup raisins, chopped.
2 tablespoons flour.
½ teaspoon cloves.
½ teaspoon cinnamon.
¼ teaspoon nutmeg.
2½ cups sifted cake flour.
1 teaspoon soda mixed with 2 tablespoons water.
½ teaspoon salt.

Cream the sugar and fat, add the applesauce and the soda which has been dissolved in the water. Mix and sift the dry ingredients and add them, with the floured raisins, to the first mixture. Beat well, pour into a greased pan, and bake in a moderate oven (350°F.) for about 35 minutes.

Main Dishes

Baked soybeans

6 servings, about ⅔ cup each

Soybeans, dry	2 cups
Boiling water	6 cups
Salt	1 teaspoon
Bacon, diced	¼ pound
Onion, chopped	½ cup
Brown sugar, packed	¼ cup
Salt	1½ teaspoons
Dry mustard	1 teaspoon
Bean cooking liquid and water	¾ cup
Light molasses	¼ cup

Boil beans for 2 minutes in water. Let stand 1 hour. Add salt. Cook 2 to 3 hours or until tender. Drain; save liquid.

Preheat oven to 325°F. (slow).

Place cooked soybeans in a beanpot or 2-quart baking dish.

Mix remaining ingredients and stir into soybeans. Cover and bake 3 hours. Remove cover during last hour of baking to reduce liquid and brown the top.

Meat loaf

6 servings 1 slice each, about 1¼ inches thick

Ground beef	1½ pounds

Egg	1
Milk	½ cup
Onion, finely chopped	½ cup
Breadcrumbs, fine dry	⅓ cup
Salt	1 teaspoon
Pepper	¼ teaspoon
Sage	¼ teaspoon

Preheat oven to 350°F. (moderate). Mix all ingredients thoroughly. Press into a 9- by 5- by 3-inch loaf pan. Bake 1½ hours.

Remove from oven; drain off excess fat.

Beef shish kebabs

6 servings

Boneless sirloin steak	2 pounds
Oil	¼ cup
Lemon juice	3 tablespoons
Dry white wine	¼ cup
Garlic powder	⅛ teaspoon
Thyme	⅛ teaspoon
Salt	1 teaspoon
Green peppers, cut in eighths	3
Boiling water	3 cups
Mushroom caps	24
Pearl onions, whole, cooked	24
Tomato sauce	8-ounce can
Brown sugar	1 tablespoon
Hot pepper sauce	⅛ teaspoon

The day before:

Cut meat into cubes. Place in bowl.

Mix oil, lemon juice, wine, garlic powder, thyme, and salt. Pour oil mixture over meat. Let stand in refrigerator for 24 hours.

The day of serving:

Drain meat; save liquid.

Cook green pepper pieces in 1 cup boiling water for 5 minutes or until almost tender. Drain.

Pour 2 cups boiling water over mushrooms. Cover. Let stand 5 minutes. Drain.

Alternate meat cubes, onions, mushrooms, and green pepper pieces on skewers.

Mix tomato sauce, brown sugar, and hot pepper sauce with remaining liquid from meat. Brush meat and vegetables with tomato sauce mixture.

Broil, turning as needed, until meat is of desired doneness.

Heat remaining tomato mixture. Serve over meat and vegetables.

Brunswick stew

6 servings, 1½ cups each

Chicken, whole or cut-up	3 pounds
Salt	1½ teaspoons
Water	3 cups
Potatoes, diced	1 cup
Frozen lima beans	1¾ cups
Tomatoes	16-ounce can
Onions, chopped	⅔ cup
Corn, frozen	1¾ cups
Salt	½ teaspoon
Pepper	⅛ teaspoon
Poultry seasoning	⅛ teaspoon
Water	¼ cup
Flour	2 tablespoons

Simmer chicken in salted water until tender. Drain, save broth. Separate the meat from the skin and bones and cut meat into pieces as desired.

Skim fat from broth. The fat can be skimmed more easily if the broth is chilled enough to solidify the fat.

Add potatoes to broth and simmer 5 minutes.

Add lima beans, tomatoes, and onions. Simmer 7 minutes.

Add chicken, corn, and seasonings. Cook 3 minutes longer.

Mix ¼ cup water with flour until smooth. Add to stew and heat just long enough to thicken, stirring as needed.

Eggs benedict

6 servings

Canadian bacon	6 slices, about 2 ounces each
Oil or fat, melted	1 tablespoon
English muffins, cut in half	3
Butter or margarine	1 tablespoon
Eggs	6
Salt	½ teaspoon
Boiling water	4 cups or more
Mock hollandaise sauce (p. 18)	1 recipe

Fry bacon in fat in frypan. Keep warm.

Spread English muffin halves with butter or margarine. Toast under broiler.

Break eggs into saucer, one at a time. Slip each egg gently into boiling salted water. Water should cover eggs. Reheat to simmering. Simmer, covered, until eggs are of desired doneness, about 3 minutes for medium.

Top each muffin half with slice of bacon; then with poached egg. Serve with mock hollandaise sauce over top of egg.

Beef stew

6 servings, 1½ cups each

Boneless stew beef, 1-inch cubes	**1½ pounds**
Fat or oil	**2 tablespoons**
Water	**3 cups**
Bay leaf	**1**
Potatoes, quartered	**3 cups**
Carrots, cut in chunks	**1½ cups**
Onions	**6 small**
Salt	**2 teaspoons**
Pepper	**¼ teaspoon**
Flour	**¼ cup**
Water	**⅓ cup**

Brown meat on all sides in fat in a large, heavy saucepan. Add 3 cups water and bay leaf. Cover tightly. Simmer about 2 hours or until meat is tender.

Add vegetables and seasonings and continue cooking, covered, about 25 minutes or until vegetables are tender. Remove bay leaf.

Stir flour into ⅓ cup water until smooth.

Stir flour mixture gently into stew; continue stirring only as needed to prevent sticking until stew thickens.

Curried pork chops

6 servings, 1 chop each

Pork chops, loin	**6**
Flour	**¼ cup**
Oil or fat, melted	**1 tablespoon**
Mushrooms, sliced, drained	**8-ounce can**
Onion, finely chopped	**⅓ cup**
Butter or margarine	**2 tablespoons**
Flour	**2 tablespoons**
Salt	**1½ teaspoons**
Curry powder	**1 teaspoon**
Milk	**1½ cups**

Preheat oven to 350°F. (moderate).

Coat chops with ¼ cup flour. Brown chops on both sides in fat.

Place chops in baking pan. Cover chops with mushrooms.

Cook onion in butter or margarine until tender. Stir in 2 tablespoons flour, salt, and curry powder. Gradually stir in milk. Cook, stirring constantly, until thickened.

Pour milk mixture over chops. Cover pan. Bake 1 hour or until chops are tender.

Lasagna

9 servings, 1 cup each

Ground beef	¾ pound
Garlic cloves, finely chopped	2
Onion, chopped	½ cup
Salt	1½ teaspoons
Red pepper, crushed, dried	⅛ teaspoon
Oregano	1 teaspoon
Parsley, dried	1 tablespoon
Tomato paste	6-ounce can
Tomato sauce	8-ounce can
Hot water	¾ cup
Lasagna noodles	6
Egg, beaten	1
Ricotta cheese	12 ounces
Mozzarella cheese, thinly sliced	4 ounces
Parmesan cheese, grated	¼ cup

Crumble ground beef into large frypan. Cook over moderate heat, stirring as needed, until beef is lightly browned. Add garlic and onion; cook until onion becomes tender. Stir in seasonings, tomato paste, tomato sauce, and water.

Cook lasagna noodles until tender, using directions on package.

Mix egg with Ricotta cheese.

Preheat oven to 350°F. (moderate).

In a 7- by 12- by 2-inch baking dish, spread layers of one-fourth of tomato-meat sauce, then three noodles, and another one-fourth of tomato-meat sauce. Top with half of each kind of cheese. Add another one-fourth of the tomato-meat sauce; then the remaining Ricotta mixture and Mozzarella cheese. Spread with remaining noodles and sauce. Top with remaining Parmesan cheese.

Bake, uncovered, 30 minutes. Cool 10 minutes before serving.

NOTE: Lasagna freezes well either before or after baking. Thaw in refrigerator. Leftover lasagna can also be stored in the refrigerator for a day or two, and tastes just as good reheated as when freshly baked.

Moussaka
(lamb and eggplant casserole)

6 servings, 1 cup each

Eggplant, pared, sliced	1 small (about 1 pound)
Salt	½ teaspoon
Flour, unsifted	½ cup
Fat or oil	¼ cup
Onion, finely chopped	½ cup
Ground lamb	1½ pounds
Dry red wine	¼ cup
Tomato sauce	½ cup
Parsley, chopped	1 tablespoon
Thyme	½ teaspoon
Pepper	⅛ teaspoon
Salt	1 teaspoon
Breadcrumbs, fine dry	½ cup
Tomatoes, peeled, sliced	2
Yogurt	8-ounce container
Egg yolks, beaten	2
Parmesan cheese, grated	¼ cup

Sprinkle eggplant slices with ½ teaspoon salt. Let stand 1 hour.

Preheat oven to 375°F. (moderate). Grease 3-quart casserole.

Dry eggplant with paper towel. Coat with half of the flour. Brown lightly in fat.

Cook onion and lamb until lamb is lightly browned. Drain off excess fat.

Mix wine, tomato sauce, parsley, thyme, pepper, and 1 teaspoon salt. Pour over meat mixture. Cook over low heat for 15 minutes.

Sprinkle half of the breadcrumbs in bottom of casserole. Arrange eggplant slices in layer on breadcrumbs. Spread meat mixture over eggplant slices. Place tomato slices on top of meat.

Beat yogurt, egg yolks, and remaining flour together. Pour over tomato slices. Sprinkle with Parmesan cheese. Top with remaining bread crumbs. Bake 45 minutes.

Braised beef and vegetables

6 servings, about 3½ ounces meat and 1 cup vegetable each

Beef chuck, boneless, ½-inch thick	2 pounds
Flour	¼ cup
Salt	1 teaspoon
Pepper	⅛ teaspoon
Fat or oil	2 tablespoons
Water	½ cup
Onions	6 small
Carrots, cut into 2- or 3-inch pieces	6 medium
Celery, cut into 1-inch pieces	3 stalks
Potatoes, quartered	6 small

Preheat oven to 350°F. (moderate). Cut meat into six serving pieces. Mix flour and seasonings; coat meat with mixture.

Heat fat in large frypan. Brown meat on both sides, turning once. Place browned meat in large baking pan. Add water, onions, carrots, and celery. Cover and bake 1 hour.

Add potatoes, cover, and bake 45 minutes longer or until vegetables are tender. Remove meat and vegetables from liquid before serving. Make gravy with liquid, if desired.

Sauerbraten

12 servings, 3 ounces each

Onions, sliced	2 cups
Lemon juice	¼ cup
Vinegar	1½ cups
Sugar	1 tablespoon
Cloves, whole	12
Bay leaves	4
Pepper	⅛ teaspoon
Salt	2 teaspoons
Beef rump roast, boneless	About 3½ pounds
Fat or oil	2 tablespoons
Cooking liquid and water	1½ cups
Cold water	½ cup
Gingersnaps, crushed	½ cup

Two days before:

Mix onions, lemon juice, vinegar, sugar, cloves, bay leaves, pepper, and salt. Place roast in bowl. Pour onion mixture over roast. Let stand in refrigerator for 48 hours. Turn roast over in bowl halfway through standing period.

The day of serving:

Remove roast from onion mixture; drain.

Brown meat in fat in heavy pan. Add onion mixture. Simmer until tender, about 2½ hours. Remove meat; strain cooking liquid.

Heat cooking liquid and water to boiling.

Mix cold water and gingersnaps. Stir into boiling liquid. Cook, stirring constantly, until thickened.

Slice roast into thin slices. Serve with gingersnap gravy.

Quiche Lorraine

6 servings

Bacon	8 ounces
Pastry shell, unbaked	9-inch
Swiss cheese, natural, coarsely shredded	1½ cups (7 ounces)
Salt	¾ teaspoon
Pepper	¼ teaspoon
Cayenne	Dash
Nutmeg	Dash
Eggs	4
Half-and-half	1½ cups

Preheat oven to 375°F. (moderate).

Cut bacon into pieces and fry until brown and very crisp. Drain well. Crumble bacon into pastry shell. Sprinkle cheese over the bacon. Mix seasonings and sprinkle over cheese.

Beat eggs and half-and-half together. Pour over cheese and bacon.

Bake 45 minutes or until lightly browned and a knife inserted into the center comes out clean.

Hamburger Parmesan

6 servings, 1 patty each

Ground beef round	1½ pounds
Salt	½ teaspoon
Pepper	⅛ teaspoon
Flour, unsifted	¼ cup

Eggs, beaten	2
Breadcrumbs, fine dry	1 cup
Fat or oil	3 tablespoons
Mozzarella cheese	6 slices
Mushroom pieces, drained	4-ounce can
Spaghetti sauce	15-ounce can
Parmesan cheese	3 tablespoons

Preheat oven to 400°F. (hot).

Gently mix ground beef with salt and pepper. Shape into six patties about ½ inch thick. Coat each patty with flour; dip into eggs. Coat with breadcrumbs. Brown patties in fat.

Arrange patties in single layer in baking pan, about 13 by 9 by 2 inches. Top each patty with a slice of Mozzarella cheese. Place mushroom pieces on top of cheese-covered patties. Top with spaghetti sauce. Sprinkle with Parmesan cheese.

Bake 25 minutes or until sauce is bubbly and cheese melted.

Vegetables

Corn pudding

6 servings, about ⅔ cup each

Frozen corn, whole kernel	3½ cups
Milk	1 cup
Eggs, slightly beaten	3
Salt	1 teaspoon
Pepper	⅛ teaspoon
Butter or margarine, melted	2 tablespoons
Sugar	3 tablespoons

Preheat oven to 325°F. (slow). Grease 1½-quart casserole.

Cook corn according to package directions. Drain. Scald milk.

Mix remaining ingredients together. Slowly add hot milk to egg mixture. Add corn. Pour into casserole.

Bake 30 minutes or until set.

NOTE: Instead of frozen corn, use two 17-ounce cans whole-kernel corn, heated until boiling and drained.

Cabbage cooked in milk

6 servings, ½ cup each

Cabbage, shredded	1 quart
Milk	1½ cups
Flour	2 tablespoons
Butter or margarine, melted	2 tablespoons
Salt	1 teaspoon
Pepper	Dash

Add cabbage to milk and simmer for 2 minutes.

Mix the flour and fat and add a little of the hot milk. Stir into cabbage and cook for 3 or 4 minutes until thickened, stirring constantly.

Season with salt and pepper.

Eggplant-tomato casserole

6 servings, ¾ cup each

Onion, chopped	1 large
Eggplants, peeled and diced	2 small
Butter or margarine	¼ cup
Tomatoes, drained	28-ounce can
Salt	1 teaspoon
Pepper	⅛ teaspoon
Corn flake crumbs	¼ cup

Preheat oven to 350°F. (moderate).

Cook onion and eggplant in fat until golden brown. Add tomatoes, salt, and pepper. Mix thoroughly. Pour into casserole and top with crumbs.

Bake 30 minutes.

Sauces

Mock hollandaise sauce

6 servings, 2 tablespoons each

Cream cheese, softened	3-ounce package
Egg, beaten	1
Lemon juice	2 tablespoons
Milk	2 tablespoons
Salt	⅛ teaspoon

Beat cream cheese and egg together until smooth. Add lemon juice, milk, and salt. Mix well.

Cook over low heat, stirring constantly, until sauce is thick and fluffy.

Salads

Jellied vegetable salad

6 servings, ½ cup each

Lemon-flavored gelatin	3-ounce package
Unflavored gelatin	1 teaspoon
Boiling water	1 cup
Cold water	1 cup
Onion, finely chopped	1 teaspoon
Salt	½ teaspoon
Green pepper, chopped	¼ cup
Carrots, shredded	¼ cup
Celery, diced	¼ cup
Radishes, thinly sliced	¼ cup
Salad greens	6 leaves

Mix flavored and unflavored gelatin. Dissolve in boiling water. Add cold water, onion, and salt.

Chill in refrigerator until mixture begins to thicken.

Gently stir in green pepper, carrots, celery, and radishes. Pour into a 1-quart mold or six individual molds.

Chill until set. Unmold on salad greens.

Luncheon chef's salad

6 servings, about 3 cups each without dressing

Head lettuce	1 medium

Desserts

Sour cream cookies

4 dozen cookies

Butter or margarine, softened	½ cup
Sugar	1 cup
Eggs, beaten	2
Vanilla	1 teaspoon
Flour, unsifted	1¾ cups
Salt	½ teaspoon
Baking soda	¼ teaspoon
Nutmeg	½ teaspoon
Sour cream	½ cup
Nuts, chopped	1 cup

Preheat oven to 375°F. (moderate). Grease baking sheets.

Beat fat and sugar together until creamy. Beat in eggs and vanilla.

Stir flour, salt, baking soda, and nutmeg together. Mix flour mixture, sour cream, and nuts with fat mixture.

Drop dough from a teaspoon onto baking sheets; space cookies about 2 inches apart.

Bake 10 to 12 minutes, or until lightly browned around the edges.

Baked pastry shell

8- or 9-inch pastry shell, 6 to 8 servings

Flour, unsifted	1 cup
Salt	½ teaspoon
Shortening or lard	⅓ cup

Cold water	**About 2 tablespoons**

Preheat oven to 450°F. (very hot).

Mix flour and salt thoroughly. Mix in fat only until mixture is crumbly. A pastry blender, two table knives, or a fork may be used for mixing. Add a little water at a time while mixing lightly. Dough should be just moist enough to cling together when pressed.

For easier handling, cover dough tightly and let stand a few minutes.

Shape dough into a ball. Roll out on a lightly floured surface until the dough is at least an inch wider all around than the piepan.

Fold dough in half for easier lifting and centering in piepan.

Smooth pastry into place, lifting edges as necessary to eliminate air bubbles.

Trim off irregular edges leaving about one-half inch beyond edge of pan; fold under to edge of pan. Shape edge into plain or fancy rim, as desired. Prick bottom and sides well with a fork before baking.

Bake 12 to 15 minutes until golden brown. Cool before filling.

VARIATIONS

Pastry shell filled before baking.—Do not prick the pastry. Fill and bake as directed in pie filling recipe.

Pastry for two-crust pie.—Double the recipe for baked pastry shell. Form dough into two balls, one slightly larger than the other. Roll out larger ball and fit into piepan. Roll remaining dough for top crust; make small slits to let steam escape during baking. Put filling into pastry-lined pan and top with second crust. Fold edges of pastry under and press together firmly to seal. Bake as directed in pie recipe.

Apple pie

9-inch pie, 6 to 8 servings

Pastry for two-crust pie (p. 21)	1
Sugar	¾ cup
Cornstarch	1 tablespoon
Cinnamon	½ teaspoon
Apples, tart, pared, sliced	6 cups

Preheat oven to 400°F. (hot).

Prepare pastry.

Mix dry ingredients lightly with apples in a bowl. Put filling into pastry-lined 9-inch pan. Top with second crust. Fold edges of pastry under and press together firmly to seal.

Bake 50 to 60 minutes or until filling is bubbly and crust is lightly browned.

Apple turnovers

6 turnovers

Pastry

Flour, unsifted	1½ cups
Salt	¾ teaspoon
Shortening	½ cup
Cold water	About 3 tablespoons
Butter or margarine	2 tablespoons

Filling

Apples, tart, pared, sliced	1½ cups
Sugar	¼ cup
Salt	⅛ teaspoon
Cinnamon	¼ teaspoon
Nutmeg	⅛ teaspoon

Mix flour and salt thoroughly. Mix in shortening only until mixture is crumbly. A pastry blender, two table knives, or a fork may be used for mixing.

Add water, a little at a time, mixing lightly. Dough should be just moist enough to cling together when pressed. Shape dough into a ball.

Roll out on a lightly floured surface until dough is about 12 by 12 inches. Dot with butter or margarine.

Fold pastry so that two sides meet in center. Press folded pastry with fingers. Fold ends to center and press with fingers.

Wrap in waxed paper and chill.

Divide pastry into six balls. Roll each ball out on a lightly floured surface to make a 6-inch square.

Preheat oven to 400°F. (hot).

Place about ¼ cup apples onto half of each pastry square about ½ inch from edges so that when top is folded over the turnover will be triangular.

Mix sugar, salt, cinnamon, and nutmeg. Sprinkle apples with sugar mixture.

Moisten edges of pastry squares. Fold pastry diagonally over apple mixture. Seal edges with a fork. Prick tops of turnovers.

Bake until lightly browned, about 25 to 30 minutes.

Gingerbread

9 servings

Shortening	½ cup
Brown sugar, packed	⅓ cup
Egg	1
Light molasses	½ cup

Flour, unsifted	1½ cups
Salt	½ teaspoon
Baking soda	¾ teaspoon
Ginger	½ teaspoon
Cinnamon	½ teaspoon
Boiling water	½ cup

Preheat oven to 350°F. (moderate). Grease an 8- by 8- by 2-inch baking pan.

Beat shortening and sugar until creamy. Add egg and molasses; beat well.

Mix dry ingredients thoroughly. Add to molasses mixture alternately with boiling water. Beat after each addition.

Pour batter into pan. Bake 35 to 40 minutes. Serve warm.

Cheesecake

9-inch cake, 12 servings

Zwieback crumbs	1 cup
Butter or margarine, melted	2 tablespoons
Sugar	2 tablespoons
Cinnamon	¼ teaspoon
Cream cheese, softened	16 ounces
Sugar	½ cup
Flour	2 tablespoons
Salt	½ teaspoon
Lemon rind, grated	1 lemon
Lemon juice	1 lemon
Egg yolks	5
Sour cream	1 cup
Vanilla	½ teaspoon
Egg whites	5

Mix crumbs, melted fat, sugar, and cinnamon. Line bottom of 9-inch spring-form pan with ¾ cup crumbs, saving remaining crumbs for top.

Preheat oven to 325°F. (slow).

Beat cheese until soft. Mix in sugar, flour, and salt. Stir in lemon rind and juice. Add yolks one at a time, beating after each addition. Add sour cream and vanilla. Mix well.

Beat egg whites until stiff. Fold egg whites into cheese mixture.

Pour mixture into pan. Cover with remaining crumbs. Bake 1 hour or until set.

Cool on cake rack. Refrigerate.

Sponge cake roll

8 servings

Cake flour, unsifted	**1 cup**
or	
All-purpose flour, unsifted	**1 cup less 2 tablespoons**
Baking powder	**1 teaspoon**
Salt	**¼ teaspoon**
Eggs	**3**
Sugar	**1 cup**
Water	**⅓ cup**
Vanilla	**1 teaspoon**
Confectioner's sugar	**¼ cup**
Filling	**As desired**

Preheat oven to 375°F. (moderate). Line a 15- by 10- by 1-inch pan with foil or heavy paper; grease.

Mix flour, baking powder, and salt thoroughly.

Beat eggs about 5 minutes until thick and lemon colored and heavy peaks cling to lifted beater. Beat in sugar 1 tablespoon at a time. Slowly mix in the water and vanilla.

Gently mix or fold in dry ingredients only until batter is smooth.

Pour into pan. Bake 12 to 15 minutes, just until center is firm when lightly touched.

Place a sheet of foil or waxed paper on a rack; sprinkle with about three-fourths of the confectioner's sugar. Turn cake onto foil or paper. Peel foil or paper from cake and quickly trim away any crusty edges. Cool on rack.

Spread cake with a filling, as desired (See note). Starting with the narrow edge, roll cake. Place seam down. Sift remaining confectioner's sugar over top.

NOTE: For the filling, use jelly or jam. Or use whipped dessert topping or sweetened, flavored whipped cream alone or with fresh blueberries or sliced, sweetened strawberries (well drained). Or fill a chilled roll with slightly softened ice cream and place in freezer until used.

Yellow chiffon cake

10-inch cake, 15 servings

Oil	½ cup
Egg yolks	4
Water	¾ cup
Vanilla	1½ teaspoons
Cake flour, unsifted	2 cups
Sugar	1½ cups
Baking powder	2½ teaspoons
Salt	1 teaspoon
Egg whites	4
Cream of tartar	½ teaspoon

Preheat oven to 350°F. (moderate).

Place oil, unbeaten egg yolks, water, and vanilla in mixing bowl, and mix well.

Mix dry ingredients thoroughly and add to liquid mixture. Beat until smooth.

Pour egg whites into large mixing bowl. Add cream of tartar. Beat until very stiff peaks are formed.

Fold egg yolk mixture gently into egg white mixture. Pour batter immediately into an ungreased 10-inch tube pan.

Bake about 1¼ hours, or until top is springy to touch.

Invert cake in pan until cool. Serve plain or topped with a lemon or chocolate glaze.

www.ingramcontent.com/pod-product-compliance
Lightning Source LLC
Chambersburg PA
CBHW081128080526
44587CB00021B/3796